How Culture Shapes Social-Emotional Development

Implications for Practice in Infant-Family Programs

by Monimalika Day, Ph.D., and Rebecca Parlakian

ZERO TO THREE
Washington, D.C.

Acknowledgments

We gratefully acknowledge those organizations whose leadership has supported the Center for Program Excellence and its publications. We also extend our thanks to the W. Clement and Jessie V. Stone Foundation for generous support of the Center's work.

Series Editor

Nancy L. Seibel, M.Ed., NCC

ZERO TO THREE Reviewers

Linda Eggbeer, M.Ed.
Emily Fenichel, M.S.W.
Elizabeth Ford
Angie Godfrey, M.Ed.
Tammy Mann, Ph.D.
Stefanie Powers, M.S.

Expert Reviewers

Maria D. Chavez, Ed.D., President, Las Mujeres
Bruce Grellong, Ph.D., Jewish Board of Family and
    Children's Services
Alicia Lieberman, Ph.D., San Francisco General Hospital
Cheryl Polk, Ph.D., Miriam and Peter Haas Fund
Harry H. Wright, M.D., M.B.A., University of South
    Carolina School of Medicine, Columbia

From Park Street Children's Center, Rockville, MD:
Farideh Beiglarbegi, Jo Farrell, and Debra Watkins

We are especially grateful for the contribution of researcher and writer-intern Ginny Lewis in the creation of this publication.

ZERO TO THREE

http://www.zerotothree.org

ISBN 0-943657-74-1

Authors: Monimalika Day, Ph.D., and Rebecca Parlakian
Series Editor: Nancy L. Seibel, M.Ed., NCC
Composition: Betsy Kulamer
Cover photo: © Marilyn Nolt
Photo credits: page 7, Rebecca Parlakian; page 11, Nancy
    Guadagno; page 17, Janelle Durlin

Suggested citation:
    Day, M., & Parlakian, R. (2003). *How culture shapes social-emotional development: Implications for practice in infant-family programs.* Washington, DC: ZERO TO THREE.

Additional copies of this monograph are available from ZERO TO THREE. Call 800-899-4301 or visit our Web site at http://www.zerotothree.org

Introduction

Three-year-old Nicholas is in foster care. He recently met his early intervention home visitor for the first time. He was being assessed for hyperactivity and attention deficit disorder, at the request of his foster mother. Nicholas had been removed from his parents' home because of neglect due to drug abuse. His foster placements had changed three times in the past year due to his frequent temper outbursts and hyperactivity. As Nicholas entered the room where his home visitor was waiting, he had a bewildered look. His eyes were wide as moons, and he was clearly shaking. He seemed utterly frightened of what might happen. As the home visitor asked him if he was a little afraid, he said (more to himself), "I am never afraid. I am afraid of nothing…I am tough."

—Adapted from Maldonado-Durán, Karacostas, & Millhuff, in press

In many societies, boys are expected to be tough. This expectation is fostered by parents and caregivers in many ways across different settings. When a 2-year-old boy falls down at his child-care center, he may be told, "Don't cry; you're strong." When he gets into a peer conflict at home and comes crying to his mother, she may respond by saying, "Don't cry. Fight back!" In a similar situation, a 2-year-old girl may be comforted and soothed—with the underlying assumption that it is okay for girls to cry. And if a girl fights back in a disagreement with a peer, she may be labeled a tomboy and told, "Girls don't hit!"

How children view themselves, how they express their feelings, and how they interpret their roles and relationships within a family and the larger society are strongly influenced by cultural values and expectations. The situation becomes even more complicated when the values and expectations at home are different from those in a child-care setting or other infant-family program. So while a little boy may be told, "Don't cry; you're strong" at home, he may hear, "It's okay to cry" when he falls down and skins his knee at child care.

As the United States—and infant-family programs across the nation—become increasingly diverse, the issue of how best to integrate families' home culture into program services has become an important question for program leaders. Culturally based differences may lead to conflict and feelings of being misunderstood or judged—for both families and practitioners. For children, unresolved differences between culture at home and in infant-family programs can result in difficulties that affect their social and emotional development. Programs that work to understand and respond to culturally based differences in the families they serve are doing much to support children's healthy social-emotional development.

This publication examines how culture shapes children's fundamental learning about themselves, their emotions and their way of interacting and relating to others. In the following pages, program leaders will learn more about how culture influences both parenting and program services. Readers will find suggestions on how to use cultural differences as an opportunity to understand themselves better, as well as the children and families with whom they work.

The sections outlined below each conclude with strategies for program staff and leaders to ensure a culturally responsive approach to services.

- The sections titled **What Is Culture?** and **What Is Social-Emotional Development?** provide working definitions of these concepts;
- **Experiencing, Expressing, and Regulating Emotions** discusses how emotional expression is affected by one's cultural context.
- **Developing Close and Secure Interpersonal Relationships** explores how culture influences the connections children establish with parents, other important adults, and peers.
- **Exploring and Learning From the Environment** examines how a child's culture shapes what and how she learns.
- **The Process of Cultural Reciprocity** presents several tools and strategies that program staff and leaders may use to resolve cultural conflicts when they arise.

What Is Culture?

There are many definitions of culture. For the purposes of this publication, we will use the one describing culture as "an integrated pattern of human behavior that includes thoughts, communications, languages, practices, beliefs, values, customs, courtesies, rituals, manners of interacting, roles, relationships, and expected behaviors of a racial, ethnic, religious, or social

> **"All people participate in both the larger, mainstream culture and smaller cultural groups."**

group" (Cross, Bazron, Dennis, & Isaacs, 1989, p. 13). Culture is transmitted through succeeding generations and is dynamic.

Three key concepts help us to understand culture:

- **values**—the relative importance of an action or thing. For example, in the United States, the mainstream culture tends to value independence.
- **beliefs**—what is accepted as the truth by a group of people. Individuals tend to be strongly attached to their beliefs and are unlikely to change them even though they often cannot offer a rationale for them. For example, one person may believe in the existence of a higher being and another may not.
- **assumptions**—a working hypothesis based on previous experience. Individuals are usually able to explain the rationale behind an assumption. They tend to be less attached to their assumptions and are more likely to change them with information and experience. For example, many parents in the United States assume that answering a baby's cries too quickly will lead to spoiling him. Upon learning that holding a crying child helps him learn to soothe himself, parents are often willing to change this assumption.

All people participate in both the larger, mainstream culture (macroculture) and smaller cultural groups (microculture). Consider a person born in the United States (macroculture), of Taiwanese descent (microculture), and the parent of a child with multiple disabilities (another microculture). Although individuals participate to varying extents in the mainstream culture, they will continue to retain attributes of their original cultural traditions (Kalyanpur & Harry, 1999). A mother may give her child the antibiotics prescribed by the pediatrician (conforming to mainstream expectations), but she may also take steps to reverse the "evil eye" that she suspects to be a factor affecting her child's health.

Years of education and experience working with infants, toddlers, and families contribute to the development of a professional culture, with its own beliefs, values, and assumptions. In some cases, the beliefs and values of our professional culture are similar to the beliefs and values of the families with whom we work. In other cases, there may be major differences between one's professional culture and a family's culture. For example, a family may believe that providers are experts and, as such, will be directive and tell them exactly what they should do. A provider, however, may wish to collaborate with the parents as equals.

The cultural influences described here create a specific context for each person—an individual culture. Human beings grow and develop within this context (Bronfenbrenner, 1977). This publication focuses on the concept of individual culture, as it provides a useful framework to help the reader understand how to work with people from cultural backgrounds different from one's own (Harry, Kalyanpur, & Day, 1999).

It is important to recognize that culture is neither absolute nor static. Changes in culture are clearly evident among immigrant groups; such changes also occur among non-immigrants, although at a slower pace. Because each person's context is individual and unique, it is of little use to learn, for example, the "African-American" approach or "Hispanic" approach to parenting and child rearing. To give culture a "deterministic role" in the lives of children or families "results in stereotyping, and stereotyping creates barriers to understanding" (Anderson & Fenichel, 1989, p. 8).

What Is Social-Emotional Development?

The social-emotional domain of development is concerned with a child's ability to experience, express, and regulate emotion and to establish loving, supportive relationships with others. ZERO TO THREE's (2001) definition of healthy social-emotional development (or infant mental health) encompasses these and other crucial skills and includes the developing capacity of the child from birth to age 3 to:

- experience, regulate, and express emotions;
- form close and secure interpersonal relationships; and
- explore the environment and learn from it,

all in the context of family, community, and cultural expectations for young children.

■ The phrase **"developing capacity"** is a reminder of the amazingly rapid pace of growth and change in the first 3 years of life.

"When Kyle was first born, it was just diaper changes and feedings. But now, at 4 months, he's all personality. He smiles and plays with me. He loves bright colors. And I swear he has a favorite lullaby. I mean, he's a real person!"

Characteristics of Culture

Culture is

➤ Learned—It is transmitted across generations through socialization and learned through one's experiences and interactions.

➤ Shared—Shared norms for behaviors, values, and beliefs characterize specific cultural groups.

➤ Ever-changing—Culture is associated with adaptation to the environment. As the environment changes, groups change to improve their ability to survive or to make maximum use of their environments.

➤ Universal—Everyone has a culture.

—Adapted from Weber & Kelley, 2002, p. 20

Kyle is showing his emerging ability to engage and interact with others.

■ Infants and toddlers depend heavily on adults to help them **experience, express, and regulate emotions.**

"I've been trying to help Shyla [2 years old] stop biting when she gets angry. We kept talking about how to 'use your words' to show you're upset. And then yesterday at play group, Ben grabbed a toy out of her hand. She turned to me and said, 'Mama, no, no!' And then she started to cry…but she didn't bite. I just gave her a big hug and told her how proud I was. Then we made our way over to Ben and talked about sharing the toys."

Shyla is showing her growing skill at substituting words for actions and regulating her emotions in appropriate ways.

■ Through **close and secure interpersonal relationships** with parents and other caregivers, infants and toddlers learn what people expect of them and what they can expect of other people.

Jayson [14 months old] was on a walk with his father when he became frightened of a neighbor's dog barking from behind a fence. "Hey, Buddy, what's wrong? Is Champy making too much noise?" Jayson turned and ran a few steps back to his father, who scooped him up in a

In the following sections, we will explore in more detail how each aspect of social-emotional development discussed here is influenced by one's culture.

Experiencing, Expressing, and Regulating Emotions

Experiencing and Expressing Emotions

Though we experience a range of emotions each day, it is rare that we stop and think about exactly what an emotion is. For the purpose of this publication, we define emotion as "the experience of a feeling (e.g., happiness, sadness) that happens together with some physiological change within the body (e.g., a hormonal or neural reaction)." We express emotions in a range of ways; these expressions include subtle behaviors, such as a small change in facial expression, and more overt behaviors such as laughing, crying, or tantrums. Verbal infants and toddlers may be able to express emotions using words as well as actions.

Early infant emotions shape and are shaped by relationships with others, especially parents. For example, adults demonstrate and teach emotional expression to infants through exaggerated facial expressions or intonation. Sometimes adults unintentionally teach children about emotional expression—as in the case of a parent whose own emotional expression is unregulated or depressed. Parents and others, such as infant-family professionals, also influence children's emotional expression in the way that they respond to infants and toddlers. For example, a baby smiles, and the adult smiles back. Note that this emotional interaction is bidirectional: How the child responds emotionally influences how the parent responds, which will influence how the child responds, and so on. Of course, individual differences abound. Children will exhibit different emotional responses to the same situation—for example, drop-off at child care—based on their culture, personal history, and temperament.

Very young children are keen observers and learn about appropriate ways to express and share emotion by watching interactions around them. Babies also look to adults to determine how they should feel in a new situation; this is

hug. "Champy startled me, too. I guess he must be feeling a little grumpy today, huh?"

Jayson is learning that, when he becomes uncertain and fearful, other people—like his father—will be there to support him. His father's sensitive response contributes to Jayson's growing sense of security, trust, and self-esteem.

■ The drive to **explore the environment and learn** is inborn in humans. Infants' and toddlers' active participation in their own learning and development is an important aspect of their mental health.

Kara [3 years old] was at the petting zoo with her parents. She was curious about the sheep. As she reached her hand out to touch, she looked up at her mother. "Go ahead, sweetie." With that, Kara stroked the animal's fur. She turned back to her mother, eyes wide, smiling, and exclaimed, "Soft! So soft!"

Kara's actions show how children learn within the context of a relationship and how they use their senses to explore the world.

called social referencing. Infants and toddlers look for cues from the trusted adults in their world: Is this scary? Should I be happy? Should I welcome this person? Is it okay to smile?

Molly, 6 months old, is starting child care in one week. Today was her first day to visit the infant room. Maryam, the head teacher, approached Molly and her mother, Tracy, with arms outstretched. "Welcome!" she said, with a big smile. Molly turned away, nestled closer to her mother, and looked up at Tracy's face with a quizzical expression. Tracy smiled back at Maryam, touched her arm, and said warmly, "It's so nice to see you again. We haven't been back since our tour last week, and I thought it might be good to stop by." Molly watched her mother closely. Then she looked back at Maryam and gave her a big grin.

Culture influences the expression of emotions. Findings of cross-cultural research suggest that basic human emotions are universal (Ekman, 1994 in Trawick-Smith, 2003). Broadly speaking, emotions such as fear, anger, and happiness are part of human interactions in all cultural groups. Variations among cultures emerge, not in the emotions that individuals experience, but in the way that they are expressed. For example, how are children taught to handle anger? Children from more collective cultures, such as Japan and China, are often taught to avoid expressing anger altogether (Slonim, 1991). This may be because of a belief that showing anger openly threatens the interdependence of the group (Pham, 1999). Children from more individualistic cultures (such as the United States) are generally encouraged to express their feelings openly, as this highlights "the separation of self from others" (Markus & Kitayama in Pham, 1999, p. 103). Beginning from birth, children learn appropriate ways of expressing emotion in their cultures and modify their affects based on cultural and family norms.

Several attributes of emotional expression tend to vary across cultures. These include the following:

■ **Animation**, or the intensity of emotional expression—

Keisha and Ashanti (both 3 years old) were negotiating who would be allowed to enter the castle they built in their child-care room. As they discussed the "castle rules," their tones of voice

and body language intensified. Jayne, their teacher, checked in to see what was wrong. The girls looked at her in surprise. They weren't arguing, they explained, just talking.

■ **Volume of speech**, or loudness—

Lei, mother of twin sons, found her home visitor, Heather, to be very loud. Her voice seemed to take up the whole room. Heather, on the other hand, always commented to her colleagues about how quiet Lei was. "She barely talks above a whisper," Heather said during a staff meeting. "You wouldn't believe how quiet that apartment is. You'd never guess two toddlers live there!"

■ **Directness of questions**—

Caroline (18 months old) and her father were chatting with Yolanda, her caregiver. "So," said Caroline's father, "Caro is pretty advanced compared to the other kids, don't you think?" Yolanda smiled but felt uncomfortable and wasn't sure how to answer. Caroline was surely very bright and had a sizable vocabulary, but to say it out loud like that—well, it felt wrong.

■ **Directness of eye contact**—

Yoko, mother of Kenji (4 weeks old), met John, her early intervention home visitor, for the first time. Kenji was referred as a result of a hearing loss that was detected at birth. Later, John told colleagues, "Mom hardly looked me in the eye once. Maybe she's really overwhelmed by the diagnosis, or maybe we just didn't click."

■ **Touching**—

Dana, a family support worker, was meeting with Tariq (8 months old) and his mother. As she approached their home, she saw Tariq's father greet a male friend with a hug and a kiss on both cheeks. He also held the friend's hand as they walked to a neighbor's home. Dana had never seen him physically express such affection with his wife. She wondered what it all meant.

■ **Use of gestures** (such as nodding or hand movements)—

Tia was listening to the nurse home visitor explain how to dose her son's asthma medication. She was a little confused, but she nodded so that the nurse would know that she was listening. Later, the home visitor thought back over her day and felt relieved that Tia understood so clearly what was going on. Other parents find the dosing pretty tricky.

■ **Physical proximity** (the physical distance or zone of personal space with which people feel comfortable)—

Eleni's mother, Sofia, approached Shawna, the head infant teacher. Sofia was asking how often the children were taken outside for a walk each day. Eleni, she explained, loved going outside. Shawna later told her colleagues, "That Sofia! She was right in my face, asking me about the outdoor play policy. I mean, step back! How rude."

Differences in how emotions are expressed do not mean that one way is right and another wrong. Though a staff member may feel that a particular way of expressing emotion is familiar, preferred, or even healthier than another way, it is important to consider the cultural context of a family's style of emotional expression. It is

> **"Differences in how emotions are expressed do not mean that one way is right and another wrong."**

also worthwhile to consider what meaning the family assigns to a particular emotion or action. For example, in the United States, it is common in some religions for family members at wakes or funerals to tell humorous stories about the deceased. This does not connote a lack of respect but is, instead, one way of grieving. In other countries and religions, however, this behavior would be seen as inappropriate or disrespectful.

Suggestions for Further Exploration

✔ Begin by observing parents and children to gather more information about their style of emotional expression. How do families interact with staff, with one another, and with other children and adults? How do parents and chil-

dren handle separations, reunions, celebrations, and conflicts? Where do families fall in the attributes of emotional expression listed above and on pages 5–6? For example, does the family seem to use direct eye contact frequently, rarely, or occasionally?

✔ Think about your own style of emotional expression. What was your experience growing up? How were emotions expressed within your family? Outside the family? What similarities or differences exist between your experiences and those of the families with whom you work?

✔ Your own reactions to families provide important information. If you feel confused, irritated, or uncertain after an interaction with a family, it is possible that there is a cultural basis for their behavior that is based on values, beliefs, or assumptions that differ from your own. Use your reactions as a reminder to take the time to reflect, ask questions, and learn more.

✔ When a family's style of emotional expression feels uncomfortable to you, stop for a moment before responding. Ask yourself: Is it damaging to the family or child in some way, or simply different? How is this style of expression understood and experienced by family members? How are my own beliefs influencing my assessment of this family?

✔ When conflicts or misunderstandings occur due to differences in communication style, use the strategies of cultural reciprocity (pages 16 through 24) to address families' concerns, articulate your own beliefs and culture, and identify an appropriate resolution.

Regulating Emotions

Emotional regulation is the ability of an infant to control and manage the effects of intense feelings. Emotional regulation is influenced by many factors, including culture, temperament, and life experiences (for example, a history of neglect or abuse). Babies rely on the emotional expressions of their caregivers to guide their own feelings. They get visual, verbal, and tactile cues that help them to regulate their emotions. In the following vignette, what is this child learning about emotional regulation?

A father is rocking his sobbing 18-month-old (who desperately wants to have another cookie but has been told no). He brushes her curls with his fingers, and whispers calming words in her ear; his expression is soft, he has a sympathetic look, and occasionally he gives her a kind smile. Soon the child's cries begin to decrease in intensity. When the father realizes this, he begins to sing "Old MacDonald," looking expectantly at his daughter when it comes time to "quack, quack." She joins in and is soon happily singing along.

PHOTO CREDIT: REBECCA PARLAKIAN

Emotional regulation is influenced by prevalent cultural norms and practices. Cultures in which importance is placed on verbal interactions tend to use words to express feelings, provide comfort, and nurture babies. Cultures that emphasize physical proximity may address these same issues through touch, holding, and carrying. Stack and Muir (1992) studied the effects of touch on babies and reported that touch could effectively communicate excitement or comfort to babies as young as 3 months old.

Learning how parents from different cultures teach very young children how to regulate emotion can lead us to questioning basic assumptions about "typical" infant behavior. For example, the average Western infant cries most frequently during the first 8 weeks of life. Then parents typically see a decrease over the next several months—with a crying peak at 6–8 weeks (Small, 1999). Infants also seem to cry more in the evening than at any other time of day. In contrast, a study of 160 Korean babies found no clear crying peak at 2 months and no cluster of evening crying (Small, 1999).

What could be the reason for this difference in crying patterns? One significant difference in parenting style in these two samples is that mothers in Korea tend to be more physically engaged with their babies than are mothers in the West. For example, the Korean babies in the sample were carried almost twice as long each day as American babies (Small, 1999). Korean mothers also respond to virtually every infant cry, whereas American mothers were more apt to let the baby "cry it out" in some cases (Small, 1999).

It seems likely that cultural differences in parenting beliefs and caregiving approaches influence how children learn to express and regulate emotions even in their first days and months of life. Parents provide their infants and toddlers with a context and example for how best to keep oneself calm and recover when emotions become too strong. Whether this is through touch or talk (or both), parents help their infants learn to regulate themselves in culturally appropriate ways.

Recommendations for Staff and Leaders

✔ Modify program practices or services to support families' beliefs about emotional expression and emotional regulation. Staff members can discuss with families how they can adapt and integrate family practices into program services. For example, for families who typically keep their children physically close as a strategy to promote children's emotional regulation, child-care professionals can use a sling or baby carrier for portions of the day to replicate the infants' experience at home. For families who may typically use a softer tone of voice to communicate, service providers can be especially aware of their own tone of voice when speaking with children and families.

✔ Ask questions and learn more about the meaning behind a family's actions or emotions. Understanding what a particular action or emotion means to the family is important information for providers. For example, in some cultures it is common for men not to be very involved in caring for a newborn. This area is viewed as the domain of the mother and other female relatives. Knowing the meaning behind a father's "backseat" role, the provider will not fall into the trap of making assumptions, such as "the father must not be very happy about the birth" or "the father is uninvolved and uncaring."

✔ Reflect on your own approach to emotional expression and regulation. Consider the attributes on pages 5 and 6, and think about how you and your staff members express and regulate emotion. It is important to create a work environment that supports diverse communication styles. One may succeed in hiring a diverse team, but if individuals feel constrained, limited, or judged for how they express themselves, a program will not be successful in retaining staff over the long term.

✔ When faced with a colleague whose communication style is one you just don't "click" with, ask yourself, "Is this person's approach damaging to the program's team dynamics, or just different? What specific elements am I having trouble with? Is this because my beliefs about communication and emotional expression are different?" Being aware of one's own beliefs and cultural influences, learning to manage one's own reactions, and reserving judgment are important skills in creating a truly multicultural work environment. Consider the vignette below:

Dr. Allen, the program director, walked into Monique's classroom and was somewhat startled to hear a voice booming across the room, shouting rather forceful instructions at Jose, who was in the process of climbing on a table. The child was also quite startled and quickly complied with the teacher's request. Monique continued her activities and gathered the children on the rug for an animated and joyous storytelling session while Jose found his way onto her lap.

Although initially put off by Monique's loud voice and strong personality, Dr. Allen recognized her sensitivity and caring as well. It was clear that she expressed warmth and affection to the children with an intensity that exceeded any expressions of dissatisfaction or disappointment. Dr. Allen believed that Monique could improve her discipline strategies, but the quality that had first turned her off—Monique's loud voice—no longer bothered her so much.

—Adapted from Donahue, Falk, & Gersony Provet, 2000, p. 75

Developing Close and Secure Interpersonal Relationships

Communication Styles and Relationship Building

Culture is a lens through which children and adults understand the rules of relationships. This lens influences issues such as how quiet or outspoken we are, how likely we are to ask questions of those we consider experts, how we state our approval or disapproval, and what information we feel comfortable sharing with those outside our family or circle of friends. Such qualities can have a major effect on how easily a provider establishes a strong relationship with children and families.

One important attribute of culture is communication style (Hall, 1977). Understanding how families communicate is critical information when trying to build a relationship with them; in fact, this knowledge forms the foundation of effective relationships.

Low-context cultures (such as those found in Western Europe or the United States) are ones in which meaning is communicated primarily through written and spoken words. Meaning is typically explicit—conveyed in a direct, linear, verbal manner.

High-context cultures (such as those found in Asia, South America, and Native American communities) tend to use a communication style in which a verbal or written message is generally ambiguous, indirect, and open to interpretation. High-context cultures rely on shared knowledge within the group to help convey meaning. The message is implicit in situational, nonverbal cues, such as body language, setting, or knowledge of the relationships involved.

The potential challenge here is clear. Families from a high-context culture may not feel comfortable verbally sharing their concerns or questions with direct service providers. Furthermore, they may be reluctant to express the concern they feel when they disagree or are confused by a particular treatment suggestion or caregiving practice. Providers who are more accustomed to a direct way of communicating may interpret this silence positively—as a sign that the family agrees and is "on board." Providers may then be surprised when the family does not follow up on suggested next steps.

When communication difficulties like this occur, both family members and providers feel misunderstood. Parents may have a sense that "this provider is telling us what to do when I know my child best," whereas providers may feel that "these parents must not care if they're not trying this new treatment." Understanding a family's communication style helps to avoid such misunderstandings. For providers, this means learning to be "fluent" in other ways of sharing and seeking information. Such flexibility helps to ensure that families' unique needs are met.

Affiliation and Noticing Differences

It was once believed that infants form close relationships only with their mothers. However, research in the past few decades indicates that babies can form close relationships with many different caregivers—fathers, grandparents, child care providers, neighbors, and so on (Waters & Cummings, 2000). The relationships that young children develop early in life promote their ability to explore, learn, and develop emotional resilience.

Even babies are adept at noticing differences among people; this awareness typically begins at birth, as a newborn recognizes his mother's smell and voice apart from those of others. Between 6 and 8 months, with the emergence of stranger anxiety, this ability to note differences among people becomes acute. As children grow, they begin the process of affiliation, or seeking out others of "their own kind." This affiliation occurs as very young children's observation skills become increasingly sophisticated and they master the cognitive skill of categorization—recognizing similarities and differences—and match-

---

Types of Interaction

A Low-Context Interaction

Ted, father of Lindsay (2 years old), asked to speak with Betsy, his daughter's child-care teacher. Ted explained that his daughter's lovey, a furry bear, was missing. Had Betsy seen it? Betsy apologized and said that she hadn't but would look in the classroom. Just then, Ted's eye was drawn to the playground. "Hey, there's her bear. Some kid is playing with it outside. Can you make sure it gets back to Lindsay?" Betsy assured him that she would.

A High-Context Interaction

Midori, mother of Nobu (2 years old), asked to speak with Betsy, her son's child-care teacher. Midori explained that her son's lovey, a fuzzy yellow duck, was missing. Had Betsy seen it? Betsy apologized and said that she hadn't seen the duck but would look in the classroom. Midori smiled faintly and thanked Betsy, but her eyes remained fixed on something over Betsy's shoulder—out on the playground. As Midori left the classroom, Betsy took Nobu in hand and walked outside to join the rest of the class. There she saw one of the other children, Sam, throwing Nobu's duck into the air and catching it. Betsy returned the duck to Nobu but wondered why Midori hadn't mentioned seeing Sam with the duck. Surely she had seen him playing with it through the window.

Questions To Think About

1. What is Ted's concern? How did he share it with Betsy?

2. What is Midori's concern? How did she share it with Betsy?

3. How are Midori and Ted's communication styles similar and different?

4. With which communication style did Betsy seem more comfortable? Why do you think this was so?

---

ing the things that "belong" together. During this time, children may react differently to different people, which may affect their ability to establish relationships. Two examples follow:

Omi, whose parents are from Iran, is entering child care at 18 months old. On his first day, Omi cried and showed great distress when he was left with his teacher, Anne, but he was easily comforted later by Hayedeh (a teacher at the center originally from Iran). She sat Omi on her lap, whispered some reassurances to him in Farsi, and sang a children's song for him in Farsi. After that, Omi would walk into Hayedeh's classroom each morning for some special time together before joining Anne and the rest of his class.

Questions to Think About

1. If you were Anne, what are some of the things you might do to build a closer relationship with Omi?
2. How could the program leader support Anne in her efforts to establish a relationship with Omi?
3. Omi's relationship with Hayedeh seems to be helping him get accustomed to child care. How can the program leader support Omi through a change in center routines or a reallocation of resources?

Tracy, a 3-year-old African-American child, and Briana, a 3-year-old White child, were playing together at child care. Tracy's mother, Caryn, was volunteering for the day. Caryn was surprised to see that Briana seemed fascinated with her daughter's curls, touching them and winding them around her fingers. Though Tracy didn't seem to mind—in fact, she giggled—Caryn found herself feeling upset by what she saw. Growing up, she had been one of the few Black children in her elementary school and had often been teased about her curly hair. Caryn later approached the girls' teacher, concerned that she hadn't intervened in what Caryn believed to be Briana's inappropriate behavior.

Questions to Think About

1. Why do you think Briana behaved the way she did?
2. What meaning do you think Caryn might be placing on Briana's behavior?
3. If you were the teacher in this vignette, how would you have responded to Caryn's concerns?
4. As the teacher, what could you do to help the girls appreciate their similarities and differences?
5. How could the teacher help Caryn understand the meaning of Briana's actions from a developmental perspective?

Between ages 2 and 3, children become openly curious about differences. This can be challenging for parents and other adults who work closely with children. As the above example shows, adults—as a result of their own history and experiences—can be tempted to view children's interest in differences in adult terms, as discrimination or racism. In actuality, this curiosity is evidence of children's growing ability to observe, categorize, and understand how their world works.

Two- and 3-year-olds talk about differences between themselves and others and begin to observe differences such as those among genders, skin colors, languages, pronunciations, or eye shapes. To the toddler anxious to categorize his world, a specific practice (e.g., pronouncing a word in a particular way) or body feature (e.g., white skin) may be seen to be "right" or "correct." Listening closely to children's early observations about differences provides rich opportunities to correct the misconceptions that children may hold about groups or individuals. These observations also create wonderful "teachable moments" to affirm identity and encourage an acceptance of diversity.

Children look to the adults in their lives for information about how to perceive and understand differences. Clearly, parents play a critical role in this learning process. It is also important that infant-family professionals remain sensitive to the messages they are sending. Consider the vignette below:

Charlotte, a new caregiver at an inner-city child-care center for at-risk children, was taking two of the children in her room to a nearby park. She held each child's hand and talked with them about what they saw as they walked—a tree, a stop sign, a fire engine. Charlotte noticed a group of teen-age boys from the neighborhood walking toward them. They were wearing their jeans low on their hips, and they looked rough. The group was taking up the whole sidewalk and talking loudly. Charlotte wasn't from this neighborhood, but she had heard about its high crime rates. Suddenly, she felt scared and tightened her grip on the children's hands. She quickly headed for the nearest crosswalk to cross the street. As she turned, she heard one of the boys holler, "Hey, lady!" She didn't turn around. Again, he said more insistently, "Hey, lady, you with the kids!" Charlotte took a deep breath and looked his way. One of the boys walked toward her. "One of your kids dropped a mitten." "Oh," said Charlotte, "Thank you."

Questions to Think About

1. What was Charlotte's assumption?
2. What might have led her to have such an assumption?

3. How might Charlotte's reaction to this situation affect the children in her care?

4. If you were Charlotte's supervisor and she shared this story with you, how might you respond?

Identity Development and Relating to Others

Very young children develop within the context of relationships. The process of developing a sense of identity, or self, begins at birth, as babies learn who they are from how people interact with them. Loving interactions make very young children feel valued, protected, and important. The positive sense of self that emerges from experiences like these gives children the confidence and resilience they need to venture out, explore their world, and be ready to learn (ZERO TO THREE, 1992).

Children's sense of individual identity is influenced by their group identities. A sense of group identity emerges when the child develops an affiliation with people whom the child's immediate family considers to be like them—such as fellow parishioners at church, other families in a play group, or members of a social club to which the family belongs.

Early in life, children learn about how others view people like themselves from the interactions they have within and outside their groups and from messages they receive in books and magazines and on television. These messages often convey powerful value judgments—good, bad, beautiful, ugly, successful, likely to fail—that are not lost on even very young children. Moreover, interviews with 2- and 3-year-olds suggest that they do not understand the representational nature of televised images; what they see on television is, to them, real (Fitch, Huston, & Wright, 1993). Thus, the sparse and almost uniformly negative portrayals of ethnic minorities on television (Palmer, Taylor Smith, & Strawser, 1993) can be particularly damaging for toddlers unable to differentiate between such images and real life.

Children who regularly see people who look like themselves depicted in a positive light begin to develop positive self-esteem, whereas children who often see images portraying people from their background in a negative manner may begin to dislike who they are (Derman-Sparks & Ramsey, 2002). Some children begin to think

PHOTO CREDIT: NANCY GUADAGNO

that they naturally belong in this society, whereas some children realize that they are viewed as "others" or outside the mainstream. When an infant or toddler belongs to a group that is less valued by mainstream society, it is especially important to provide them with experiences that will help them develop a strong and positive group identity.

Cultural Continuity

A successful staff-child relationship has many elements. Nurturing, responsive, individualized care enhances the rapport between infants and direct service providers. Cultural continuity also supports the development of a high-quality relationship between child and provider. Cultural continuity refers to "the ongoing transmission [from one generation to the next] … of experiences, beliefs, values, and practices [shared] by a [cultural] group" (Chang & Pulido, and Nugent in Sanchez & Thorp, 1998, p. 5).

> **When infant-family services are linked to families' home cultures, the process of cultural continuity is supported.**

Continuity from home to infant-family settings offers children an "emotional and intellectual base of support from which children can negotiate the new or unfamiliar" (Sanchez & Thorp, 1998, p. 6).

When infant-family services are linked to families' home cultures, the process of cultural continuity is supported (Sanchez & Thorp, 1998). The relationship with the provider feels familiar to children when their families' values, beliefs, and practices are respected and supported. The provider is able to replicate the familiar ebb and flow of interactions, routines, and rituals that the child experiences with the important adults in her life, and within her culture. The result is that the child experiences less stress and her home culture's values are reinforced (Kuhn in Kaiser & Sklar Rasminsky, 2003).

What happens when program services are not congruent with families' home culture, or when there is cultural discontinuity? Providers may subtly, even unconsciously, subvert children's cultural identity by communicating indifference or disrespect of the family's culture and child-rearing practices (Anderson & Fenichel, 1989). Children lose a crucial and basic frame of reference in these environments. Much of what they have already learned in the context of their home culture may no longer apply. Their talents, competencies, and abilities may not be recognized or appreciated, and behavior that was

acceptable at home may be suddenly and inexplicably inappropriate (Kaiser & Sklar Rasminsky, 2003). Children may find themselves at a disadvantage as compared to their more acculturated or mainstream peers. A sense of being less competent than their peers affects children's developing sense of who they are. Children in environments like these may experience feelings of isolation, alienation, and conflict (Chud & Fahlman in Kaiser & Sklar Rasminsky, 2003).

In many infant-family programs, direct service providers may not share the culture of the families with whom they work. In addition, they may be challenged to meet the needs of families representing a wide range of cultural groups. A good guiding principle for practitioners working in diverse environments is to "pay attention to the beliefs that parents hold, especially when parents differ in background from those offering advice" (Goodnow, 2001). To resolve the differences that may arise, staff members can use the tools and strategies of cultural reciprocity to build collaborative and effective partnerships with families (see pages 16 through 24).

Recommendations for Staff

✔ Choose books, music, toys, visual images, and foods that reflect children's home cultures and languages. Enlarge photographs of children and their families, neighborhood activities or street fairs, and community landmarks. For older toddlers, ask parents to contribute empty boxes of common foods for the house area and ensure that dolls reflect a variety of cultures. In home visiting programs, staff members can create a toy library, in which home visitors can borrow toys and games that reflect the cultures of the families they are visiting.

✔ Learn how a child refers to wants and needs—one language may be used for milk, while another may be used for juice. Promote staff's familiarity with frequently used words or terms (such as "play," "bathroom," "yes," and "no") because this knowledge is helpful for staff and reassuring for children.

✔ For group settings, involve all children in activities. Young children whose home language is not English may feel uncomfortable participating because they do not understand the conversation and play of those around them. Staff can work to reduce children's isolation by asking parents for translations of important words and concepts and by alternating English-centered songs, stories, and games with those featuring other languages.

Recommendations for Leaders

✔ Discuss cultural differences among staff members in supervisory meetings or in facilitated team meetings. Do staff members feel that their cultures and beliefs are supported? Before program leaders can expect staff to be sensitive and responsive to families' cultures, they must work to create a program culture in which all team members are themselves respected and supported.

✔ Find ways to help families whose first language is not English feel welcome and able to participate in the program. For example, whenever possible, translate any signs, memos, or materials into families' home languages. Ask families to teach staff and other families how they celebrate important traditions and holidays. Help staff learn key words and phrases in families' home languages.

✔ Provide opportunities for staff members to strategize about how to meet families' needs best or accommodate families' requests. This can be accomplished through regular staff meetings that provide staff with opportunities to discuss the challenges and successes that they are currently facing in their work. Dialogue among staff also helps colleagues to learn from one another and to access the expertise that is a part of every infant-family professional team.

✔ Seek to hire staff who are representative of the families served. This gives families the opportunity to make known the beliefs and values that are important to them, helps staff members understand the families and children better, and contributes to the delivery of individualized services. Hiring practices are a powerful strategy for developing a culturally competent staff. Though it is beyond the scope of this publication to discuss recruitment strategies in detail, this issue remains an important one for program leaders to consider.

✔ Remember that diversity is important even when the children and families being served are fairly homogeneous. Exposure to new groups helps everyone in the program to become more open and accepting of differences. Program leaders should think beyond the traditional definition of a "diverse" staff and seek to hire qualified staff members who will enrich the diversity of the program's team in all areas—including men and people with disabilities.

Exploring and Learning From the Environment

There is a reciprocal relationship between culture and development: As children learn new skills, they are learning about their culture, and the cultural background of a child often determines which new tasks are learned. For example, when a Lakota Sioux grandmother helps her 3-year-old granddaughter to do beadwork, the child is not simply enhancing her fine motor skills by learning to string beads, she is also learning her tribe's history, beliefs, and traditions.

Parental Goals

Each culture identifies and teaches children a set of highly valued skills, beliefs, abilities, and personal qualities best suited to the needs of that community—these are called *parental goals* (Ferber in Small, 1999). Parental goals reinforce cultural rules and convey the key elements of a particular family's culture to the next generation (Small, 1999).

Parental goals also profoundly shape the interactions that parents have with their children. For example, in Japan, babies are viewed as separate entities who need to be integrated into the family, or brought "into the fold" (Small, 1999). This is a parental goal, and it is promoted through behaviors such as holding babies, keeping them in close bodily contact, and encouraging mother-baby interdependence. In addition, babies almost universally sleep with their parents. In contrast, many parents in the United States believe that a baby is a highly dependent being; a common parental goal is to increase a child's independence, or ability to do things on his own. Practices like putting babies to sleep separately from parents and using bouncy seats and swings as ways to help children soothe themselves can be seen as linked to this parental goal of independence.

The existence of parental goals reminds us that just as there is a picture of "typical" development for infants and toddlers—including typical time frames and skills—there is also great variation across individuals, families, and cultures. Parents set goals for their children based on their expectations of which tasks are important for children to learn and how quickly children are expected to learn them.

When staff members encounter a parenting practice that they don't understand or don't initially agree with, it is important to understand the meaning of the behavior from the family's perspective. What role does this practice have in the family's culture? Why is it important to the family? Why have they chosen to use this parenting practice or approach? By asking questions in a value-neutral way, staff can put parent's child-rearing beliefs in a cultural context

and begin to see them as part of a cohesive whole, rather than as isolated practices.

The Importance of Routines

Routines profoundly shape children's early learning. They are an important context through which cultural knowledge is transmitted from one generation to another. A routine that is taught by an important member of one's caregiving group (e.g., a parent) provides an example of the culturally appropriate way to handle a particular situation or complete a particular task. For example, does the parent feed her child oatmeal with a spoon or offer her rice to be eaten by hand?

Being included in routines helps a child feel affiliated with the group: "I am part of this group. I am like the other people in this group." Watching others perform the same routine creates a powerful motivation to imitate the behavior: "I can participate in this experience. We share something important." Finally, routines

---

Teachable Moments:
Understanding the Learning That Happens
in Different Activity Settings

Cynthia, an early intervention provider, was meeting with the Coates family. She arrived on time at their single-family home at the end of a cul-de-sac in an affluent suburban neighborhood. Mrs. Coates greeted Cynthia at the door and led her to the dinning room. Kylie, her 2-year-old daughter, was sitting in a high chair drinking from a small cup of milk. Kylie turned the cup upside down and started pouring milk on the table. Her mother picked up a sponge, shook her head a little, and said, "It's messy to let a baby learn how to feed herself."

Amy, an early intervention provider, pulled her car in front of the Wilson family's apartment in an inner-city working class neighborhood. Amy walked upstairs and knocked on the door of the family's apartment. Mrs. Wilson greeted her, saying, "How are you doing? We're eating dinner." Charlie, a 2-year-old boy, was sitting in a high chair. Mrs. Wilson put a bowl of cereal and milk in front of him and went to the kitchen to start some coffee. Charlie ate

a little and then stirred the milk vigorously with his spoon, spilling a good bit on the carpet. "Stop playing with your food! You need to eat, so you can grow up healthy!" Mrs. Wilson shouted from the kitchen. Then she came into the dinning room and stroked Charlie's cheek while saying, "Charlie-boy, you can't play with food." Mrs. Wilson turned to Amy and said, "I guess he doesn't understand how hard it is to put food on the table."

Questions To Think About

1. What might be the primary goals for each family during feeding?

2. What are the values reflected in their words and actions?

3. How do you think their social class may have influenced their goals?

4. How would you feel working with the first family? The second family?

give a child a sense of continuity and consistency: "I know what will happen now. I can anticipate and understand what will happen next. The world is a sensible, ordered place." From a social-emotional perspective, the predictability of routines also provides children with emotional stability: "I can trust that my needs will be met, and I feel safe in knowing who, where, and when" (Butterfield, 2002).

One of the most important ways that a family and a community can aid a child's development is by maximizing the teachable moments that emerge through daily routines. This natural process of learning by doing, seeing, and saying is taking place largely without conscious awareness. For example, when a mother in the United States drops her toddler off at child care in the morning, she is probably not thinking that this routine teaches her child many things about their family's culture: that women work, that cars are the primary mode of transport, that the use of car seats is a social norm (and legal requirement), that their chosen method of child care is by non-family members in a setting outside the home. Yet all these messages (and others) are embedded in this daily routine.

Activity settings are the social settings within which everyday routines take place. Children's activity settings are "not a deliberate curriculum; they are homely and familiar parts of a family's day: preparing meals, eating dinner, clearing up, ... watching television, getting ready for school, and dozens of mundane settings in which adult-child interaction is embedded" (Gallimore, Goldenberg, & Weisner, 1993, p. 1). Keep in mind that the same activity may have a different meaning or purpose, depending on the cultural background of the family.

How can infant-family professionals use what they know about a family's activity settings in their work? By understanding a child's context—the activity settings in which they live their lives—providers can find creative ways to ensure that services reflect families' existing routines and activities. For example, in a Muslim family for whom mosque is an important activity setting, speech-language therapy for a 3-year-old with a language delay might entail saying prayers with his father or learning brief sections from the Qur'an. For a family living on a farm, a child's physical therapist might build on the family's existing routines and ask that his par-

ents take him on a walk each day to the mailbox at the end of their very long driveway.

Recommendations for Staff

✔ Use families' routines as a starting point for providing services or suggesting interventions. Families often prefer that infant-family services reflect their daily routines and their families' activity settings—and, by extension, their culture. For example, when faced with making a choice about infant-toddler early intervention services, parents of children with disabilities

> ❝Routines are an important context through which cultural knowledge is transmitted.❞

"prefer interventions that are easy to do, *fit into their daily lives*, and emphasize children doing and learning things that *help them be part of family and community life* [italics ours]" (Bruder & Dunst, 1999/2000, p. 35).

How effective are such integrated services, compared to interventions that occur outside a family's routines and activity settings (such as speech therapy at a clinic)? Researchers have found that using daily routines and experiences as the context and inspiration for services (e.g., maximizing "teachable moments") actually results in "rich learning environments" for very young children (Bruder & Dunst, 1999/2000, p. 34). For infant-family professionals, this means taking the time to learn about the families with whom they work—including learning more about their cultures, their goals for their children, and their daily routines. This knowledge provides a necessary context for any discussion of services and helps providers to individualize services from the beginning. In the rare instances in which it is simply not possible to incorporate a family's routine or practice into program services, it is important to use the strategies of cultural reciprocity (see pages 16 through 24) to discuss the situation with parents.

Recommendations for Leaders

✔ Help staff members understand how their own cultures (including their parental goals and daily routines) shape their approaches to working with families.

✔ Provide opportunities for staff members to reflect on their own cultures and the diversity in the program through one or more of the following activities:

▇ Discuss common child-rearing practices from staff members' home cultures at a staff meeting. Focus on daily routines such as eating, sleeping, and playing.

▇ Ask staff members to think about when a child "should" accomplish the following:
- be able to complete simple tasks around the house (e.g., picking up her clothing);
- be able to feed himself;
- sleep through the night;
- walk;
- exhibit self-control (e.g., not touch something forbidden, like a lamp); and
- be toilet trained.

▇ Discuss how beliefs about these milestones are a reflection of staff members' own cultures, history, and experiences.

▇ Ask staff members what children are learning through routine activities such as diaper changing, hand washing, and snack time.

▇ Create opportunities for staff members to share important holiday celebrations with colleagues.

▇ Use staff meetings as an opportunity to discuss the challenges and successes that staff members are encountering with families. Ask colleagues for ideas and suggestions on next steps.

▇ Brainstorm about some of the activity settings that staff members remember from their own childhoods. How are these the same as or different from those of the families they serve? What implications does this have for the staff's work with families?

▇ Consider what additional support staff members may need to replicate families' activity settings. For example, many Native American programs use cradle boards. Infants are swad-dled and then wrapped and tied into a cradle board. Though it is a comfort to the infants and how they sleep best, it takes a little time for child care providers to go through the routine. Staff members may, therefore, need additional support at the beginning of nap time to ensure that this routine goes smoothly. Seeking reliable volunteers, such as volunteer grandparents from the community, may be one answer to this dilemma.

The Process of Cultural Reciprocity

Throughout this publication, various strategies for supporting children's social-emotional development—in the context of their home cultures—have been presented. What can providers do, however, when a cultural difference between a family and provider is negatively affecting their relationship?

Professionals can use the process of cultural reciprocity to examine cultural differences, establish a shared understanding, and build a stronger working relationship with families. Cultural reciprocity is a four-step process initiated by the provider that requires awareness, communication, and negotiation of culturally based beliefs, values, and assumptions. This approach assists professionals to address culturally based differences and identify mutually agreeable solutions. It is a two-way information-sharing process, meaning that families and professionals each share information about themselves, their cultures, and their beliefs to develop a common understanding of the problem (Kalyanpur & Harry, 1999). This process of give-and-take, each party listening and learning from the other, helps parents and providers to move beyond their differences and focus instead on understanding and compromise.

The values underlying the process of cultural reciprocity are mutual respect, collaboration, and reciprocity. *Mutual respect* refers to the acknowledgment that both parents and providers contribute an equally valued perspective to the dialogue. *Collaboration* describes the emphasis placed on partnership and the sharing of decision-making power that is inherent in this model. *Reciprocity* refers to the need for understanding, compromise, and open-mindedness that is integral to resolving any challenges that may arise.

Because the process of cultural reciprocity addresses each family situation as unique, it avoids the trap of developing solutions based on stereotypes. Instead of offering providers a "recipe" of how to work with a specific "type" of family, it provides infant-family professionals with a conceptual framework to examine cross-cultural communication on a case-by-case basis.

Cultural reciprocity includes the four steps described below. These steps can be used together or independently, depending on the circumstances. Together, they outline a strategy that providers may use to understand better the antecedents of a cultural conflict. They can also be thought of as four separate tools to help staff and leaders understand infant or parent behavior in the context of the infant's and parent's culture and to support the provision of culturally responsive services.

Step 1: Self-Awareness— Learning About Our Own Cultures

Self-awareness is the first and most important step in developing the ability to work with other cultures (Harry, Kalyanpur, & Day, 1999). Everyone has a culture, but often we are not aware of how our culture influences our attitudes, habits, and behaviors. It is especially difficult for people who belong to the dominant cultural group to examine their cultural stance because their beliefs and values are largely reflected in the people and institutions around them. As a result, some mainstream Americans may think that they do not have a culture (Lynch & Hanson, 1992). Interacting with people from various cultures and experiencing situations in which one is in the minority helps to dispel this myth.

As babies, we absorb our families' cultural values through observations and interactions with the important adults in our lives—in most cases, our immediate family. So a good place to begin thinking about our cultural identity is by examining our family heritage. Gathering information from our oldest family members (through stories or letters) is one strategy. Family stories can be supplemented by photographs, journals, family videos, and personal diaries (Lynch & Hanson, 1992). The personal experiences, jobs, and education of older generations also help us to understand the roots of our family cultures.

PHOTO CREDIT: JANELLE DURLIN

Our cultural values, beliefs, and assumptions are also influenced by membership in other groups, for example, our nationality, religion, profession, and class (among others). In the United States, the following values and assumptions may be said to describe the mainstream culture (Lynch, 1992):

1. the importance of individual and personal privacy;
2. a stated belief in the equality of all individuals;
3. informality in interactions with others;
4. an emphasis on the future and change, leading to progress;
5. the belief in the general goodness of humanity; and
6. an emphasis on the importance of time and punctuality.

17

Service providers who believe that progress is possible may become frustrated working with families who believe that their current situation is their destiny. Similarly, providers who do not subscribe to the typical North American values and beliefs described above may find it difficult to understand the culture of the infant-family program. They may, in turn, be challenged to meet the needs of families who seek continued change and personal growth. The process of cultural reciprocity helps infant-family professionals resolve such cultural conflicts.

Step 1: In Practice

Sue, a nurse practitioner, was visiting the Lopez family, whose newborn son, Eduardo, was diagnosed with Down syndrome. She had come to do an initial assessment and talk to the family about the community resources available to them, including early intervention. When she arrived at the house, she was shocked to find that the family was not interested in enrolling their son in early intervention. They were adamant about first consulting a curandero (folk healer) to see if their son's condition could be cured. Sue assured them that it could not be—it was a genetic condition and permanent. The family was resolute. Sue was frustrated, thinking to herself, "Okay, if you want to use a witch doctor, go ahead!"

But when she got to her car, she had calmed down. She spent the drive home thinking about this visit and feeling bad about how it went. She considered her own frame of reference: growing up as a member of the mainstream culture, then attending college and nursing school where, again, her culture was the predominant one. She hadn't even heard of folk medicine until moving to the Southwest. She and her family had always used Western medicine exclusively.

The Lopez family agreed to another visit. Sue began by apologizing for her approach the last time. She then asked the family questions: What were their beliefs about health and their thoughts about their son's condition? What was their first meeting with the curandero like? She wondered aloud if it would be possible to embrace both the traditional and Western approaches, that is, schedule a meeting with an early intervention professional (Sue promised to find one who was fluent in Spanish), as well as consult a curandero. The family agreed that this plan might work best for them and their son.

Questions to Think About

1. Have you ever encountered a cultural practice that you felt was wrong?
2. Why did you feel that way?
3. How did you handle it?
4. If you could do it over, would you handle this situation the same way?

Step 2: Looking Outside—Learning More About Other Cultures

Infant-family professionals can use many tools to understand better the child-rearing values, beliefs, and assumptions of families. Some of these tools include the following:

■ **Conversation**—Though it seems an obvious strategy, it is not always easy to ensure a value-neutral tone when discussing a family's practices or a program's policies. Hearing directly from families, however, remains the most effective way of learning more about their cultural perspectives. Open-ended questions are usually nonjudgmental and encourage the respondent to provide a wealth of information (e.g., "How are you toilet training your child?" rather than "Isn't toilet training a 6-month-old a little early?"). If it is necessary to engage a translator or a bicultural person to ensure effective communication, discuss this possibilty with the program supervisor or director.

■ **Observation**—When a child-rearing practice seems different from what a staff member expects or believes, it is important that staff members find an opportunity to observe the child and family in a natural environment (such as the home or a playground). By getting a sense of the daily life of a family, staff members are in a better position to understand the family's perspective. Family videos and photographs can also sometimes provide rich information about the family's culture (e.g., how a family celebrates milestones such as birthdays or holidays).

■ **Information**—By obtaining information about another culture from various sources, staff members can begin to understand the meaning or significance of various actions, habits, and rituals. Sometimes it is helpful to read about a cultural group; staff may also consult a person from that culture—preferably a colleague—to learn more about commonly held beliefs and values.

For example, you may ask a colleague who shares the Indian background of the family you're working with, "How do you toilet train children back home?" It is, of course, important to maintain families' confidentiality in these instances, as is the case with all discussions of families in the program.

■ **Reflection**—Because we filter all information through the lens of our own cultures, it can be helpful to reflect on what we have seen and heard to help us understand better the families we serve. On their own, staff members can think about the situations they've encountered with families and write their thoughts in an experience journal. Using the example of toilet training, a staff member could brainstorm all the assumptions that she has about toilet training, (e.g., it doesn't begin until age 2 or 3, it involves a potty seat, it takes up to a year). Alternatively, staff members can use team meetings or regular meetings with a supervisor (like reflective supervision, see sidebar) to understand better the cultural dilemmas that they encounter in their work.

Because beliefs about child rearing are so embedded in culture, judgments about what is right or wrong often come quickly, almost reflexively. These reactions can be hard to counter because we are usually so certain that one way is the right way. Reflection is important in these situations because it helps us develop the skill of self-awareness. The knowledge of what we bring to our work with families—our own beliefs, assumptions, and values—helps us to approach families as partners. We learn to articulate our own cultural stance, listen nonjudgmentally to theirs, and respond appropriately. Such an approach honors the diversity of families and helps to ensure that program services are relevant and meaningful to parents and children. When this happens, families are apt to participate more fully in services, which contributes to more effective developmental outcomes.

Step 2: In Practice

The Lopez family is meeting with Maria, the early intervention specialist assigned to their family. Maria does not make any suggestions or recommendations in this first visit. She simply talks with the family and watches them together. She sees that Eduardo (two months) is a loved member of a large, boisterous family. As

What Is Reflective Supervision?

"Reflective supervision is supervision that focuses on learning from work with families, that is supportive and collaborative, and that occurs on a reliable schedule. It is characterized by active listening and thoughtful questioning by both supervisor and supervisee. Reflective supervision can take various forms, for example, individual supervision, group supervision, or peer supervision" (Parlakian, 2002, p. 2).

the youngest, he has family members of all ages anticipating his needs and responding quickly to his cries. He is held constantly, either in his sisters' arms or nestled in a sling as his mother cooks and walks about the house. Much is made of his being the only son in this family of seven.

Maria also hears the family's story of immigrating to the United States after intense fighting in the family's home country destroyed their village. She asks Eduardo's mother about his birth and hears how the hospital didn't have a translator in the delivery room, how as Eduardo was born, he was rushed out of the room while his mother and father were left to wonder what could be wrong. Maria listens to the family discuss their first, disappointing meeting with Sue, the nurse practitioner, and their second, more encouraging visit. Eduardo's mother also explains how the family is consulting a curandero about their son's condition.

When she returns to the office, Maria talks with a colleague who is from this family's home country to learn more about commonly held beliefs and practices. She thinks about how her own upbringing outside the United States, as well as her education at U.S. schools and colleges, has influenced her outlook. She begins to write down what may be important to the Lopez family in receiving services and decides that she will share this list with them during her next visit and ask for their thoughts on it.

Questions to Think About
1. What are some questions you could ask a family you're working with that would give you additional information about their child-rearing practices, beliefs, and values?
2. What are some questions you could ask a staff member or colleague that would

For example, the leaders of a program with a long history of funding instability may be reluctant to make needed infrastructure investments, even after receiving a large, multiyear service contract from the state. This organization's culture, characterized by fiscal conservatism, has shaped its leaders' decision making.

Professional culture also influences our beliefs, actions, and decision making. For example, an early childhood professional working with toddlers may believe that it is important for children to have lots of opportunities for free play and discovery; this freedom ignites in the child a love of learning. A family may disagree, questioning why their child isn't being better prepared for school by learning letters and numbers. In the culture of the early childhood profession, it is a common belief that play prepares children for school in many ways. In the sandbox, children learn the rudiments of math and science, while in the book corner and the imagination area, children develop language skills and a love of words. From the perspective of this family, however, play is a separate activity from school preparation.

It is important first to recognize and then acknowledge the important influence that program culture and professional culture have on infant-family services. Step 3 of cultural reciprocity then asks providers to explain the cultural practices, beliefs, and values of their program and profession to the families with whom they work.

By articulating the cultural beliefs behind program services, staff members can give parents the information they need to make choices for their children. This openness on the part of staff also helps families to negotiate the program and the service delivery system with greater ease; their service options—and the reasons these options exist—are clear.

The ability to recognize what aspects of the program reflect the mainstream culture (and are not simply assumed to be the "normal" or "right" way of doing things) is a critical skill because it helps you first *recognize* the influence of culture in your program and then *explain* these culturally based beliefs and practices to families. To convey this information in a way that is meaningful to families, staff members can take a flexible approach based on families' communication styles. This means showing sensitivity to whether the family uses a high-

enhance your understanding of their cultural context?

3. What is it like for you when you and your doctor disagree about appropriate medical treatment? Thinking about this might help you imagine how a family may feel when their strategies are ones with which you disagree.

Step 3: Explaining Why— Communicating Information About Our Own Cultures

Everything—from the routines and procedures used at work to the next steps or services we suggest to families—is influenced by the culture of our program and the culture of our profession.

context (less direct) or low-context (more direct) communication style and modifying one's own style accordingly. For example, if a family who is uncomfortable with a direct style is asked if they have any questions during a training session on nutrition, they may remain silent. However, if they are also encouraged to jot down questions (which are then given to the presenter and answered anonymously), this family may be more likely to share what is on their minds.

Step 3: In Practice

As Eduardo turns 3 months old, his mother, Rosa, must return to work. He will be attending a center-based child-care program on a part-time basis and spending the rest of the time with his grandmother and sisters. While at child care, he will also receive early intervention services. Eduardo's mother is signing the contract to enroll him in the program today, but, before doing so, decides to take a few minutes and peek into the infant room. What she sees there disturbs her. Babies are left on the floor by themselves, while their teachers sit close by—close enough to pick them up, surely! How terrible it must be for those children!

Later, when Rosa approaches the head teacher to ask about what she sees, Laura explains (and a colleague translates):

"We do hold the children, just not all the time. When a baby is feeling sad, or lonely, or frustrated, we always hold them. And, of course, we always pick them up if they start to cry. But we try to balance that with time to play, too. Also, I know from my studies that children develop muscles in their necks, arms, and legs through activities like floor time. The research has found that playing on the floor gives babies opportunities to develop these muscles. This might be important for Eduardo, because children with Down syndrome often have low muscle tone.

There are only two of us for six babies. We can't be everywhere at once, and sometimes a baby can't be held right at that moment. When that's the case, we usually talk to the baby until we can get over to pick her up. They don't have to wait long, just a minute or so. But I want you to know that we try our best! We really love these babies." Laura invites Rosa to spend some time in the classroom so that she can see how the staff members interact with the children.

Questions to Think About

1. If you were Laura, how would you have felt when Rosa asked her question about holding babies?
2. When you have a strong reaction to a family member (either their personal style, a particular practice they're using, or the way they interact with you), what strategies do you use to stay calm?
3. How did Laura explain to Rosa what was going on in the classroom?
4. How can you find out more about the reasons behind a parent's requests?

Step 4: Coming Together— Collaborating With Members of a Different Culture

Once staff members understand the family's viewpoint and have explained their own cultural values to the family, they can begin to address the dilemma at hand. Together, the staff member and the family negotiate and collaborate to identify a solution. Key components of this step include the following:

■ **Flexibility**—Begin by generating a range of different options, rather than focusing on what will be the best solution. Often what turns out to be best is a combination of several solutions. When families make suggestions that staff members believe to be unworkable, it is important to keep these feelings in check and to avoid reacting negatively. This shuts down the process of collaboration. (Also, there are many creative ways to accommodate a family's needs; while brainstorming in an open-minded way, you may identify a great new idea.) In these situations, sometimes it helps to take a deep breath and say, "Let's think about this." Follow through by making an effort to understand the family's request and thinking about ways to incorporate it into program services.

■ **Sharing power**—Collaborative work requires the dominant group to share decision-making power with other, less-empowered partners. In a service delivery system, professionals have traditionally been in the more powerful position of making decisions. It is important in discussions with families that staff consciously and actively share this power. This means learning to be comfortable with letting the family lead.

21

Cultural Reciprocity with Colleagues

Many infant-family programs not only serve a diverse group of families but also have a very diverse staff themselves. The issues of culture, communication style, parental goals, activity settings, and dealing with differences discussed in this publication are equally applicable to families and to infant-family professionals. Because this is a complex topic, we cannot fully address it in this publication. However, below are four critical issues for program leaders to consider as they work to create a program culture that is open, inclusive, and supportive of all staff.

➤ **Consider each staff member's culture, temperament, and personal history.** Just as staff members are asked to provide individualized services to families, program leaders, too, must get to know each staff member and establish a unique relationship with each individual. This effort helps to create the kind of mutual, respectful, and collaborative relationships that characterize a culturally sensitive work environment.

➤ **It is important to discuss differences.** Just because an issue hasn't come up doesn't mean that it's not there. For example, a staff member may feel hurt and marginalized because colleagues (good-naturedly, they think) tease her about the food she brings for lunch.

Or a staff member may be frustrated by the fact that the center's "welcome back" sign is only in English, not Spanish. Another may be upset that she needs to use vacation time to observe the Jewish high holidays.

➤ **Being able to talk about how a person's cultural context influences the way she approaches her work is an important way that program leaders can provide support to staff members.** Leaders can help this happen by ensuring that staff members have access to a safe place—and a safe relationship—within which they can discuss these sometimes uncomfortable, sometimes difficult issues. Reflective supervision is one strategy that program leaders can use to create opportunities for discussions of this nature to develop.

➤ **Cultural reciprocity strategies can be used with colleagues as well as with families.** At times, conflicts occur with colleagues. Sometimes these are, at their root, caused by differences in cultural beliefs, values, and expectations. Using the four steps of cultural reciprocity honors each person's beliefs and experiences and gives each person an equal responsibility for finding a solution.

▪ **Restating and clarifying**—When staff members don't understand or don't agree with what a family member is saying, it may help to *restate* what they believe they heard or to ask questions that *clarify* what the family has said. True collaboration entails understanding. To resolve their shared dilemma, both staff members and family members must understand one another's beliefs, values, ideas, and suggestions.

Step 4: In Practice

As Eduardo begins child care, the issue of carrying and holding babies comes up again. Rosa finds that she just isn't comfortable with the amount of time Eduardo spends on the floor playing. Rosa reiterates her belief that children feel loved when they are held a lot. Keeping babies close not only makes them feel safe, but

it makes them feel cherished as well. Her Eduardo is a little king; he is a dear baby, and Rosa wants to be sure that he feels as cared for while she is gone as when she is with him.

Laura listens to Rosa and lets her know that she understands how Rosa feels. She explains again her own challenges in the room—her responsibilities to two other children in addition to Eduardo, her own belief in the need for independent play, and how she has learned that children need to have opportunities to develop stronger neck, arm, and shoulder muscles. She invites Rosa to think together with her about the possible solutions to their dilemma.

Rosa calls from home and asks if she could bring in a sling for Laura to use. Laura responds that it's a wonderful idea: "I can carry him in the sling during the morning. Then after lunch he can

*play a little on the floor. How does that sound?"
Rosa agrees that that sounds like a good compromise. She'll bring in the sling the next day.*

Questions to Think About
1. How did Laura respond to Rosa's request?
2. How do you think Laura's response made Rosa feel?
3. What are some other possible solutions that would meet both Rosa's and Laura's needs?

Real Life Is Complicated

Situations arise in infant-family work in which, after much discussion and creative problem solving, it is not possible to identify an option that meets a family's need. In these situations, staff and leaders need to focus on the following:

- communicating to the family that they fully appreciate the family's concern;
- explaining why they are not able to honor the family's request;
- exploring alternatives with the family; and in rare cases,
- helping families to locate programs that are more closely aligned with their beliefs and practices.

For example, on pages 22–23, there is a vignette in which a provider agrees to wear a sling for part of the day. What if, perhaps, this was not possible? What if the provider felt the physical demands of carrying a growing 3-month-old—along with holding other children when they were upset or wanted cuddling—felt overwhelming? Together with the program leader, this staff member could begin to articulate her concerns to the parent:

"I understand that it is important to you that Eduardo be held as often as possible. You've told me this is one of your parenting beliefs, and I see that you are almost always holding him yourself. Unfortunately, I worry that I won't be able to use the sling as you've asked. I am just not able to carry two babies at once, and if I am wearing Eduardo in the sling, that means I can't carry any of the other children in the room. And that is an important part of my job. Because I know how strongly you feel about Eduardo being held, I promise that I will make it a priority to hold him whenever I can. And I will be sure to put him to sleep in my arms at nap time."

With this suggested solution, the staff member is able to retain elements of the parent's request, while acknowledging her own limits. All programs must walk the tightrope of balancing individual requests, while maintaining quality services for all children. Think about this tightrope walk while reading the following vignette:

Rachel, 3 years old, came home from child care one day feeling very upset. When her mother asked what was wrong, she explained, "I want to eat the good food!" Her mother was confused, "What do you mean? Didn't you like your lunch today?" Rachel said, "It wasn't good. Not like everyone else. Theirs looked better." Now her mother understood. Their family had requested a kosher selection for Rachel, but she was the only one in her class with that menu choice. Her mother wondered how it felt for Rachel to be the only one with a separate meal. "I don't want to eat the special food!" said Rachel. "I don't want this yucky kosher stuff!" Rachel's mother began to feel upset. She didn't want Rachel to feel bad or deprived because of their family's decision to keep kosher. At the same time, how could they avoid it if all the other kids were eating something different? She decided to talk to Rachel's caregiver, Joan, the next morning.

Joan explained that she had little authority over the center's menus. "But isn't there anything we can do so that Rachel doesn't feel as if she is the odd one out?" asked her mother. Joan was empathetic but didn't have any suggestions. "Our food service company sets up the menus, and special meals come separately. I'm not sure what we can do. I don't want you to think that Rachel's lunch tastes bad. It's just different." Rachel's mom knew that Joan was right, but she just didn't feel good about how this conversation went. Although the family had chosen this child-care center because it was close to home, Rachel's mom began to wonder if they had made the right choice. "Maybe we should look into switching to the child-care program at the Jewish Community Center," she thought. "Then Rachel won't feel so alone."

Questions to Think About
1. How does cultural continuity (or discontinuity) influence Rachel's experience in child care?
2. How does the staff member's response influence her relationship with Rachel's mother?

infants, toddlers, and their families. These early experiences affect children's abilities to establish relationships with others, express and regulate emotions, and learn more about their worlds.

Infant-family professionals who are working to support the ongoing growth and development of both children and families may not always find it easy to understand families' different practices and incorporate them into program services. When these differences occur, staff can use the four steps of cultural reciprocity to share the responsibility for identifying solutions with families. Using these tools, professionals and parents can come together and identify the practices that support children's social-emotional development. Joining hands across two cultures, parents and providers can, together, hold a child.

3. If you were Joan's supervisor, what might you have done or suggested if she had told you about this dilemma?

4. What are some possible solutions to this dilemma?

Conclusion

The cultural context in which a baby develops offers a rich opportunity for providers and program leaders to understand and support very young children's social-emotional development. In a modern society, infants are influenced not only by their home cultures but also by the culture of their providers and infant-family programs.

Culture has a profound influence on parenting styles and the nature of services offered to

References

Anderson, P. P., & Fenichel, E. S. (1989). *Serving culturally diverse families of infants and toddlers with disabilities.* Washington, DC: National Center for Clinical Infant Programs.

Bronfenbrenner, U. (1977). Toward an experimental ecology of human development. *American Psychologist, 32,* 513-531.

Bruder, M. B., & Dunst, C. J. (1999/2000). Expanding learning opportunities for infants and toddlers in natural environments: A chance to reconceptualize early intervention. *Zero to Three, 20*(3), 34–36.

Butterfield, P. (2002). Child care is rich in routines. *Zero to Three, 22*(4), 29–32.

Cross, T., Bazron, B., Dennis, K., & Isaacs, M. (1989). *Towards a culturally competent system of care: Volume I.* Washington, DC: Georgetown University Child Development Center, CASSP Technical Assistance Center.

Derman-Sparks, L., & Ramsey, P. G. (2002). *"What if all the kids are white?": Multicultural/anti-bias education with white children.* Retrieved October 7, 2003, from http://www.rootsforchange.net/pdfs/A5B_Eng-WhatIfAll(A).pdf

Donahue, P. J., Falk, B., & Gersony Provet, A. (2000). *Mental health consultation in early childhood.* Baltimore: Paul H. Brookes.

Fitch, M., Huston, A. C., & Wright, J. C. (1993). From television forms to genre schemata: Children's perceptions of television reality. In G. L. Berry & J. K. Asamen (Eds.), *Children and television: Images in a changing sociocultural world* (pp. 38-52). Newbury Park, CA: Sage Publications.

Gallimore, R., Goldenberg, C. N., & Weisner, T. S. (1993). The social construction and subjective reality of activity settings: Implications for community psychology. *American Journal of Community Psychology, 21*(4), 537–560.

Goodnow, J. (2001). Commentary: Culture and parenting: Cross-cutting issues. *International Society for the Study of Behavioural Development Newsletter, 1*(38), 13–14.

Hall, E. T. (1977). *Beyond culture.* New York: Anchor Books.

Harry, B., Kalyanpur, M., & Day, M. (1999). *Building cultural reciprocity with families: Case studies in special education.* Baltimore: Paul H. Brookes.

Kaiser, B. & Sklar Rasminsky, J. (2003). Opening the culture door. *Young Children, 58*(4), 53–56.

Kalyanpur, M., & Harry, B. (1999). *Culture in special education: Building reciprocal family-professional relationships.* Baltimore, MD: Paul. H. Brookes.

Lynch, E. W. (1992). Developing cross-cultural competence. In Lynch, E. W. & Hanson, M. J. (Eds.) *Developing cross-cultural competence: A guide to working with young children and their families.* Baltimore: Paul H. Brookes.

Lynch, E. W., & Hanson, M. J. (1992). *Developing cross-cultural competence: A guide to working with young children and their families.* Baltimore: Paul H. Brookes.

Maldonado-Durán, M., Karacostas, V., & Millhuff, C. (in press). Transcultural issues in child mental health: Working with children and families in the Midwest of the United States. *L'Outre: Revue Transculturelle.*

Palmer, E. L., Taylor Smith, K., & Strawser, K. S. (1993). Rubik's tube: Developing a child's television worldview. In G. L. Berry & J. K. Asamen (Eds.), *Children and television: Images in a changing sociocultural world* (pp. 143-153). Newbury Park, CA: Sage Publications.

Parlakian, R. (Ed.). (2002). *Reflective supervision in practice: Stories from the field.* Washington, DC: ZERO TO THREE.

Pham, T. (1999). The influence of gender and culture on the relationship between emotional control and well-being. *Berkeley McNair Research Journal, 7,* 99–114.

Sanchez, S. Y., & Thorp, E. K. (1998). Discovering meanings of continuity: Implications for the infant/family field. *Zero to Three, 18*(6), 1–6.

Slonim, M. B. (1991). *Children, culture, and ethnicity: Evaluating and understanding the impact.* New York: Garland Publishing.

Small, M. (1999). *Our babies, ourselves: How biology shapes the way we parent.* New York: Dell.

Stack, D. M., & Muir, D. W. (1992). The effect of manipulating adult tactile stimulation during an interaction of 5-month olds' affect and attention. *Child Development, 63,* 1509–1525.

Trawick-Smith, J. (2003). *Early childhood development: A multicultural perspective.* Upper Saddle River, NJ: Merrill/Prentice Hall.

Waters, E., & Cummings, E. M. (2000). A secure base from which to explore relationships. Retrieved October 7, 2003 from http://www.psychology.sunysb.edu/attachment/online/waters_cummings.pdf

Weber, J., & Kelley, J. (2002). *Health assessment in nursing.* Philadelphia, PA: Lippincott Williams & Wilkins Publishers.

ZERO TO THREE. (1992). *Heart start: The emotional foundations of school readiness.* Washington, DC: ZERO TO THREE.

ZERO TO THREE. (2001, December.) Infant Mental Health Task Force. *Definition of infant mental health.* Retrieved August 27, 2003 from http://www.zerotothree.org/imh

Additional Resources

Fenichel, E. (Ed.). (1994). Cross-cultural studies of child development: Implications for clinicians. *Zero to Three, 15*(2).

Fenichel, E. (Ed.). (1999/2000). What do we expect? A cross-cultural look at parents' and professionals' expectations for infants and toddlers—and each other. *Zero to Three, 20*(3).

Fenichel, E. (Ed.). (2002). Routines and rituals in the lives of infants, toddlers, and families. *Zero to Three, 22*(4).

Gonzalez-Mena, J. (1993). *Multicultural issues in child care.* Mountain View, CA: Mayfield Publishing Company.

Mangione, P. L. (Ed.). (1995). *Infant/toddler caregiving: A guide to culturally sensitive care.* Sacramento, CA: California Department of Education.

Peace Corps Information Collection and Exchange. (n.d.). *Culture matters: The Peace Corps cross-cultural workbook.* Retrieved October 7, 2003, from http://www.peacecorps.gov/wws/culturematters/workbook.pdf.

Pedersen, P. B., Draguns, J. G., Lonner, W. J., & Trimble, J. E. (Eds.). (2002). *Counseling across cultures* (5th ed.). Thousand Oaks, CA: Sage Publications.

Pipes McAdoo, H. (Ed.). (1993). *Family ethnicity: Strength in diversity.* Newbury Park, CA: Sage Publications.

Rogoff, B. (2003). *The cultural nature of human development.* New York: Oxford University Press.

Sharma, D., & Fischer, K. W. (Eds.). (1998). *Socioemotional development across cultures.* San Francisco, CA: Jossey-Bass.